HELP IS ON THE WAY FOR:

Tests

Written by Marilyn Berry
Pictures by Bartholomew

CHILDRENS PRESS ™
CHICAGO

Childrens Press
School and Library Edition

Copyright ©1985 by Marilyn Berry
Institute of Living Skills, Fallbrook, CA
All rights reserved.
Printed in the United States of America.
ISBN 0-516-03238-0

Executive Producers: Ron Berry and Joy Berry
Producer: Ellen Klarberg
Editors: Nancy Cochran and Susan Motycka
Consultants: Kathleen McBride and Maureen Dryden
Design: Abigail Johnston
Typesetting: Curt Chelin

So you have to take another test.

Hang on! Help is on the way!

If you have a hard time

- understanding tests,
- studying for tests, and
- taking tests...

...you are not alone.

Just in case you're wondering...

...why don't we start at the beginning?

WHAT IS A TEST?

A test is a set of questions that measure a person's knowledge or skills in one or more areas.

A test does *not* measure a person's intelligence. It does *not* determine whether or not a person is smart.

The major purpose of a test is to determine what you know and what you don't know about a specific subject.

The purpose of a test is *not* to punish you or hurt you in any way. Tests are given for your benefit.

WHY ARE TESTS SO IMPORTANT?

Here are just a few reasons:

Tests can provide you with valuable information about yourself. They can show you
- how much you have already learned,
- what you need to learn, and
- in what areas you need extra work.

Tests can provide your teacher with valuable information about you. They can show your teacher
- if you understand what is being taught,
- if you are ready to move on to new material, and
- if you need special help in certain areas.

WHAT IS IN A TEST?

Tests are made up of one or more of the following types of questions:

1. True or false questions require you to read a statement and decide if it is true or not true.

2. Matching questions require you to match items from one list with the items of a second list.

3. Multiple choice questions require you to read a question or statement. Then you must choose an item from a list that will best answer the question or finish the statement.

4. **"Fill-in-the-blank"** questions require you to fill in the missing word or words in a sentence.

5. Short-answer questions require you to answer a question using one or two sentences.

Write down the definition of zombie and use it in a sentence.

A zombie is a person who is believed to have died and been brought back to life. Since I stayed up all night to study for this test, I feel like a ZOMBIE.

5. **Essay questions** require you to answer a question or series of questions in a paragraph or more.

Who were the Beatles? What were the names of the people in the group? List some of their major accomplishments.

The Beatles were a group of musicians from England who became popular in the 1960s. The group had four members: George Harrison, John Lennon, Paul McCartney, and Ringo Starr. They performed many hit songs, most of which written by Lennon and McCartney. Some of the

CLASSROOM TESTS

For the most part, you will take two types of tests in school: quizzes and major tests.

Quizzes are short tests that cover small amounts of material. They usually do not count as much as major tests, but they are important and should be taken seriously. Some teachers schedule quizzes on a regular basis. Other teachers surprise their classes with "pop" quizzes.

The main purpose of quizzes is to make sure you are doing your daily assignments and understanding the material. The best way to study for a quiz is to

- do your classwork and homework carefully,
- do your best not to fall behind,
- go over material you don't understand with your teacher, and
- review recent material on the days you have no homework.

Major tests are longer than quizzes and cover large amounts of material. They are usually given at the end of a unit of study or at the middle and end of each grading period. These tests most often count for a big part of your grade. Teachers generally announce these tests far in advance so you will have plenty of time to study.

The purpose of major tests is to find out if you have learned the material that has been taught. Preparing for this type of test requires some time and effort. However, studying for *and* taking major tests can be easy if you take it one step at a time.

STEP ONE: GETTING ORGANIZED

To get started, you will need to gather some important information.

Gather the Test Information.

Make up several test information sheets and keep them in your notebook or desk at school. When your teacher announces a test, fill in as much information as you can. Don't be afraid to ask your teacher questions about the test. Your test information should include these things:

Test Information

Subject_____ Date of Test_____

Type of Test_____

% of Final Grade _____

What material
Will be Covered _____

Chapters in textbook_____ Notes_____
Homework_____ Study Questions

Past Quizzes & Tests_____

Additional Information_____

Gather Your Study Material.

Gather together all the material you will need to study and review for the test. This should include all the things that are listed on your test information sheet. Don't waste time with material that will not be covered on the test.

Check Your Study Material.

Once you have gathered together your study material, make sure it has all been completed and corrected.

- Complete any missed reading or homework assignments.
- Correct any wrong answers on past quizzes or tests.
- Get any information that was discussed on a day you were absent. Ask the teacher or a classmate.

Organize Your Study Material.

Your studying will be easier if you organize your material and review small amounts of information at a time.

- Divide your study material into major topics.
- Clip together all the study material that is related to each topic.
- Make up a study sheet for each topic. List all of the study material that should be reviewed when you study each topic.

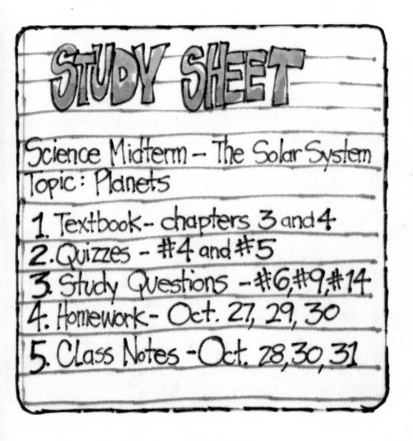

STUDY SHEET

Science Midterm – The Solar System
Topic: Planets

1. Textbook – chapters 3 and 4
2. Quizzes – #4 and #5
3. Study Questions – #6, #9, #14
4. Homework – Oct. 27, 29, 30
5. Class Notes – Oct. 28, 30, 31

Plan Your Study Time.

To plan your study time effectively, you will need to make up a test calendar. Keep the calendar on your desk at home and record all test dates as they are assigned. When you have all the information you need, set up a study plan.

- Decide how many days you have to study for the test.
- Determine how much time each day you will need to study in order to cover all the material.
- Assign a topic to each study session.

Record your study plan on your test calendar.

Test Calendar

1	2	3	4	5	6	7
				Finish Science Reading	Finish Science Homework	Study Science Topic 1 2:00-4:00
8	**9**	**10**	**11**	**12**	**13**	**14**
	Study Science Topic 2 4:00-5:00	Study Science Topic 3 6:00-7:00	Study Science Topic 4 4:00-5:00	Science Review All Topics 4:00-6:00	Science Midterm	
15	**16**	**17**	**18**	**19**	**20**	**21**
		Study Math 6:00-6:30	Study Math 6:00-6:30	Math Quiz		
22	**23**	**24**	**25**	**26**	**27**	**28**

YOU MAY WANT TO TURN THIS SIDEWAYS.

STEP TWO: STUDYING FOR THE TEST

Before You Begin a Study Session...

- Lay out all the study materials you plan to cover. Remember, you will be reviewing only a part of your study material at each study session.
- Get a package of 3 x 5 note cards. As you study, you will be summarizing important information in your own words and writing it down on the note cards.

Review Your Reading Assignment.

For most subjects, the textbook is the major source of information. That is why it is a good idea to begin your study session by reviewing the reading assignments in your textbook. If you have kept up with your reading, you should not have to completely reread the assignments. Instead, you can review by skimming the material and going over the questions at the end of each chapter.

Skimming the reading material involves looking over the chapters and writing down the important points. Important points are easier to find when you include these things in your review:

- Introductions and summaries
- Headings and sub-headings
- The topic or summary sentence in each paragraph
- Any words in special type
- Illustrations and their captions
- Maps, graphs, charts, and diagrams

When you see an important piece of information, put it in your own words and write it down on a note card. Use only one side of the card and limit the information to one complete thought.

The questions at the end of each chapter of your textbook make excellent study questions. Any information covered in these questions is important and could be on the test. Review each question by using the following method:

- Read the question carefully.
- Go through your note cards to see if you have already written down the answer to the question. If not, go back through the chapter to find the correct answer.
- Summarize the answer in your own words and record it on a note card.

Review Your Homework and Class Notes.

Your homework and class notes will probably include some of the same information you read in your textbook. You do not need to record this information a second time. Try using this method for review:

- Go through your homework one item at a time.
- Check your note cards to see if this information has already been recorded. If not, summarize the information in your own words and record it on a note card.
- Do this with each item in your homework and your class notes.

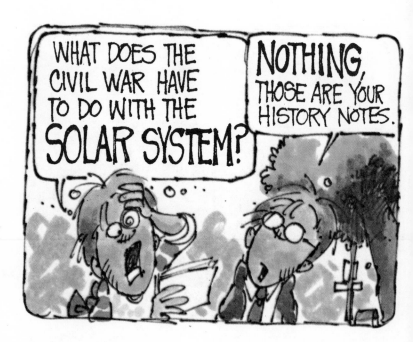

Review Study Questions, Past Quizzes, and Tests.

Study questions and the questions on past quizzes and tests are very important. They have already been chosen by your teacher as important items. You will get the most out of these questions if you do these things:

- Read through each question and its answer carefully.
- Write out each question on a note card.
- Write the answer to the question on the other side of the note card. Be sure you copy the information accurately.

Make Up Sample Questions.

You can take your studying one step further by making up sample questions.

- Look at your test information sheet to see what kind of questions will be on the test.
- Take each note card and read the information carefully.
- Turn the note card over and make up one or two questions using the information on the other side.

By now, you should have all the important information on one topic recorded on note cards. Repeat this process for each major topic.

Study Your Note Cards.

You never know when you will have some extra time to study your note cards. You may want to keep them with you. There are several ways to study your note cards.

- Read the information on the front side of the note card and try to memorize as much information as you can.
- Read the questions on the back side of the note cards and try to answer them.
- Have someone else ask you questions using the note cards.

Additional Study Tips

- If there is any information you do not completely understand, talk to your teacher about it.
- Be sure to concentrate as you study. Just reading through your note cards is not enough.
- Look up any words you do not know and write the correct spelling and definition on a note card.
- Write down on note cards any important details that should be memorized, such as names, dates, and vocabulary words and their correct spelling.

STEP THREE: TAKING THE TEST

If you have prepared properly for a test, you already have an advantage. You can get the most out of your hard work by following some simple test-taking tips.

Before the Test...

- Get a good night's sleep. Do your best to avoid last minute cramming.
- Eat a good breakfast on the day of the test.
- Be on time to class.
- When you get to class, don't talk to friends about the test or continue to review your note cards. Instead, try to concentrate on relaxing.

When You Get the Test...

- Write your name on each page of the text.
- Listen carefully to all instructions from the teacher.
- Look over the whole test, and read all the directions before you begin.
- Make a mental note of the hardest and the easiest questions.
- Look to see which questions count the most and the least.
- Quickly decide how much time you should spend on each section of the test. Be sure to allow time to check your answers.
- If there is anything you don't understand, ask the teacher to explain.

As You Take the Test...

- Before you begin a section of the test, reread the directions *carefully*.
- Write as neatly as you can.
- Answer the easiest questions first.
- If you can't answer a question, put a check by it and come back to it later.
- Use your time wisely. Don't waste a lot of time on questions of little value.
- If there is no penalty for guessing, try to answer every question.
- Don't change answers unless you are sure the new answer is correct.
- When you have finished, go over your answers and look for mistakes, such as misspelled words, punctuation, and unanswered questions.

More Test-taking Tips

Here are some tips for each type of test question.

True or False Questions
- Read each statement carefully.
- If any part of a statement is false, the *whole* statement is false.
- Look for absolute words, such as "always" and "never." These statements are *usually* false.
- Watch out for negative statements. They can be tricky.

Matching Questions
- Read the directions carefully.
- Determine if the answers can be used only once or more than once.
- Match the items you are sure about first.
- Cross out all answers as you use them if the answers can be used only once.
- Try to make a sentence out of each match. If it doesn't make sense, it probably isn't right.

Multiple Choice Questions

- Read each question carefully.
- Look for grammatical clues within the question.
- Think of a possible answer before you read the choices.
- Read all the choices carefully.
- Cross out any choices that are obviously wrong.
- From the remaining choices, pick the best possible answer.
- Test the answer by adding it to the question and reading the completed statement.

"Fill-in-the-Blank" Questions
- Read each question carefully.
- Try to choose the best possible word.
- Use correct spelling.
- Check your answer by reading the completed sentence. Be sure it makes sense.
- Count the number of blanks. Be sure to supply an answer for each one.

Short Answer and Essay Questions

- Read the directions carefully.
- Look for key words, such as ''define,'' ''compare,'' ''list,'' and ''describe.'' Make sure you answer each part of the question.
- Think about your answer before you begin writing. Try to organize the answer in your mind.
- Jot down key points you will want to include in your answer.
- Underline important facts in your answer.
- Support your points with examples.
- Write neatly.

STEP FOUR: FOLLOWING UP ON THE TEST

After your test has been graded and returned to you, it is important to do some follow-up work.

Review the Test

- Go over the questions on the test.
- Write in the correct answers to any questions you missed.
- Ask your teacher about questions you did not understand.
- Look for errors in grading. You should never lose points because the teacher made a mistake.

Interpret the Test

There are several questions you should ask yourself as you look over the test.

- Why did I do well on the test?
- Why did I not do well on the test?
- Did I study enough?
- Did I understand the material?
- Did I make careless mistakes?

Learn From the Test

If you did poorly on a test, there are several things you can do.

- Talk to your teacher and ask for extra help.
- Try to set aside more time for studying.
- Save your corrected test for future studying.
- Learn to live with your grade. A low grade doesn't mean you *can't* learn the material. It just means that you haven't learned it *yet*.

If you did well on the test, reward yourself.

STANDARDIZED TESTS

There will be times in school when you are required to take a standardized test. These tests allow you to compare your knowledge with the knowledge of other students your age across the country. There is no way to study specifically for this type of test. However, you can keep in mind that the more knowledge you gain in school, the better chance you will have of doing well on a standardized test. Use many of the test-taking tips as you answer the questions.

WARNING!

If you do the things in this book...

...you might get better grades on your tests.

THE END

About the Author

Marilyn Berry has a master's degree in education with a specialization in reading. She is on staff as a producer and creator of supplementary materials at the Institute of Living Skills. Marilyn is a published author of books and composer of music for children. She is the mother of two sons, John and Brent.